True events followed by confirmed occurrences Me
and internet quote searches

Scriptures from KJV, public domain

CLARITY

MANIFESTATION & RESULTS

SUPERNATURAL OCCURRENCES, VISION & DREAMS DECEPTION, LIES & MISFORTUNES

Charmaine M Overton

Printed in the United States of America

Cover design by Hemingway Publishers

ISBN: Printed in the United States

Published by Hemingway Publishers

www.hemingwaypublishers.com

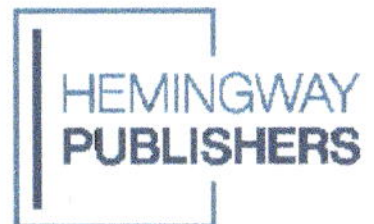

About the Author

Charmaine M Overton is the oldest sibling of her 2 brothers. She is a mother of 5 grown up children, Grandmother of 3 and Auntie. She has prophetic ablities and it has helped her stay humble. She has a jack of all trades style.She is very gifted 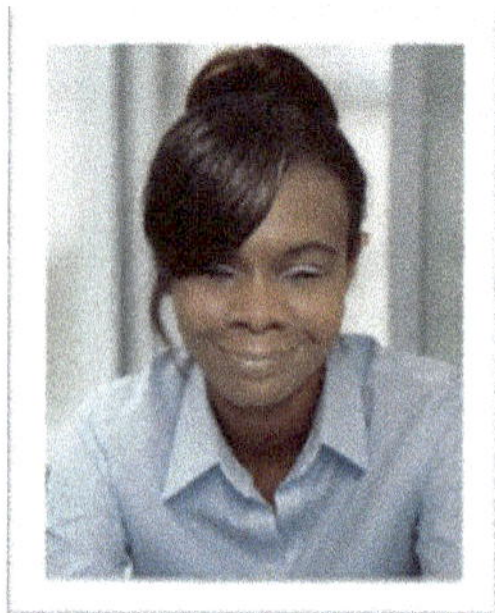 and Talented. She is very spiritual and knowledgeable. People know her of her big free spirited heart for helping the homeless and those in need. When she is able to do so. She has stuggled much and have not had it easy. The struggles life was part of her skills of solving problems and words of encouragement to those that need it. She doesn"t view the world the same as others. With her real insight for the world keeps her at bay. Hoping that others like her will not be sad, hurt and feel alone anymore. She loves people and speaking is a passion she possesses.

When I was II years old, I had given my life to Jesus through spoken confession and clarity in church in front of others and God. I have to tell what happen before then, I was on punishment for jumping out the window to go stay at a friends house. But, I wanted to go to church and my mom said no. I mean it was serious and

I was upset. I was feeling sad and wanted to kill myself. I then went to the kitchen and found the biggest knife in the kitchen drawer and took it in the bedroom with me. I was convicing myself to do it and I put the knife to my neck and moved my hand to cut and I heard a voice. Called out my name Charmaine don't do it, I have great purpose for you. I looked around the room and dropped the knife because I was confused and scared. Is that the voice of God I asked myself still scared I picked up the knife and brought the knife back to the kitchen and put it back into the kitchen drawer. Then ran out the back door. The rest is history.

Table of Contents

Amos 3:7

Surely the Lord GOD will do nothing, but he reveals
his secret unto his servants the prophets.

The Age of 9

I remember the TV sat on the floor and was so big in my eyes, shaped like a dresser. When turning the button to get to a channel, if you miss it, you got it. To turn it again. Lol, one night, my Grandmother and I were watching the Brady Bunch, and I came out and said I was going to have 5 children. Without notice, my Grandmother told me to go to bed.

The next day, we were watching Soul Train. Don't remember what group was singing. And I heard something like (your firstborn is going to be by a famous singer, son) I didn't tell my grandma that one until it happened 10 years later. God works in mysterious ways. That's why we shouldn't judge anyone. We all have a path that is designed by God.

God knew I was not going to be married when I had her, and he still spoke to me and allowed me to keep hearing.

11 years old

When I was 11 years old, I had given my life to Jesus through spoken confession and clarity in church in front of others and God. As a saved young lady, this was hard because I didn't really have anyone to confide in. My dreams and my visions were so real. I would see it happen so clearly and evident. I tried to get help, but no one listened. The Preacher could not see, and neither could my Grandmother who introduced me to the church. I was born with heart issues and was the first grandchild on both the mother and father's side of the family. At a very young age, under 5 years old, my Grandmother had the biggest Bible I can remember, and I was so attached to it. I grabbed it every day and looked at the beautiful pictures of Angels, bible characters, and Jesus on the cross for hours.

Being a saved Christian teenager had so many obstacles. It was just hard and challenging. What I went through it's sad. My mom wasn't in the church, so I was treated differently among all the other children in the church and even as an adult. Just Because, people are saved in your family doesn't mean they understand you and you're calling. Then there are Preacher's and leaders that couldn't see. This becomes the start of failure in many of the churches.

The Negative Folks

I can remember lying in my crib or bassinet. My eyes were blurry, and I was hearing voices over me, but I did not know what they meant or what was being said. This I found out later in life. I figured it out and realized that negative words were being spoken without my knowing. Because negative words were spoken over my life, it had an impact on my life without me even knowing. The negative energy starts early when the devil will use your family because they are close to you. We tend to believe in people we don't think that are not going to harm us mentally. When they speak, we really believe them, and that hurts a lot. We are sponges when we are children, and that is the only time that the enemy has a chance to trick us by putting wrong thoughts in our heads. I believe that fully.

Cousin got shot in the
heart and lived

My firstborn in April was now 3 months old. We went to NC to see my mom. During the visit, after a few days, I was up and couldn't sleep one particular night. I knew something was wrong, and I just embraced what my mind was experiencing. It's going to be alright. Early in the morning, I was thinking about many things. Then, around 6 am-8 am I was still up. A cousin came running to tell my mom that one of our cousins just got shot in the heart or near the heart. Either way, it is still not good. My mom jumped up in fear, and I immediately said he was going to be fine. My cousin and mom looked at me like I was crazy.

My cousin emphasized he was shot in the heart, and I said I heard you, and I said he is going to live. Five years after the shooting, I saw him, and he gave me the hardest hug ever and said thanks, cuz. It is because you believed.

My daughter hit him for the hug because she didn't understand, and we laughed. This is your cuz. This is the year 2023, and he is still alive.

God Spoken to me about a Man/Son Aug 1994

We have been praying for the New England Prophetic Conference in 1994-1995 until it started. I got visions and dreams that month in August. I will never forget how God really loves me, and He is with me. August 1995 was the beginning of a significant sign and wonders in my life that was only revealed to me. I was reading my Bible as I would do every evening after putting my girls to bed.

This particular evening, I was walking toward the bedroom, and I heard, "Let this mind be in you as Christ Jesus." Now, I'm the only one up. I thought it was just me thinking it. So, as I was walking towards the living room, I heard it again. Ok, I said if I hear this again, then I know it's speaking to me and trying to tell me something.

A few minutes later, I heard it again as I was going toward the kitchen to read. I said Yes, Lord, I hear you and I was asked a question. The question was, what do you want your husband's name to be? Now I am like surprised and have no answer. I grabbed the phonebook and looked at the white pages. But immediately, I heard my cousin Lamar's name and said I don't really like that name, but ok I said with acceptance. Then the Spirit of the Lord said what do you want his Last name to be, I opened the white pages of the phone book, and I opened up to the B's and saw Bryant.

So, I spoke and said my husband is Lamar Bryant. A week later, I went through similar things, smiling and trusting in my spiritual relationship. I would have another visit during my study time, and I was told I was going to have a son and to name him Immanuel (God is with Us), and he would be in heavenly places. I was like, WHAT is going on? Is this really happening to me?

On Christmas 1994, walking through the church doors, I saw a nice young man to look at. I smiled with my daughters beside me, and he said hello as well. I proceed to the sanctuary. I didn't know who he was, and that was the first time I saw him in the church, and I was raised in this church. A few days later, we had choir rehearsal. He was there, and I was told he was one of the deaconesses' grandsons, and she was in the choir. Not long after, he came to speak to me, and I was blushing like crazy. Yes, I was, and it looked like he was doing the same.

He gave me his Grandmother's phone number, and I immediately said no out of fear because I didn't know how they felt about me and having 2 children already, but she came out of the office smiling and looking at us.

Now, he came to me first. We called each other and talked for hours. I must confess he has been the only man I ever stayed on the phone until we fell asleep until this day. I must say and be clear. He had a nickname, so I never knew his actual real name right away. I asked his real name, and he just came out and told me Lamar Bryant. I smiled on the phone but never told him what I heard. Didn't want to appear crazy and desperate. He left for college to be an architect in Denver, Colorado.

We became close friends during that time he was in Connecticut. He came to me and said I was coming back to get you. Years went by, and he got married, and other incidents happened surrounding his life. We saw each other later, but my interest wasn't there anymore, and he lost interest in me long before me. God did not lie to me, He revealed it and brought it to pass. We have choices, and we must make the right choices from the beginning, or it will not work out

New England Prophetic Conference 1995

What a powerful word that just came forth from Brian Keith Williams. I began to see angels flying around in the sanctuary, and then I saw a baby boy also with the angels. I was in another dimension so powerful.

The moment had ended, and I was inspired to meet the man of God and shake his hand for that awesome gift. As I was looking and debating if he would have a second to give me even a handshake. People were already running to shake his hand. So, I quickly got over my fear and approached the Man Of God . To my surprise, he shook my hand as well as using his other hand and shook his head, as you have seen it too in agreement.

1999 - My son is born

Prophecy comes to Pass I got married in 1998 and got pregnant on my honeymoon. Yes, Immanuel was conceived right after my wedding. There was so much going on before he was born, many attacks from the church members. Let me tell you this, there was no sex before the marriage. Amen to that. God began to show me how he was going to look. Yes, it is hard to believe, but he did show me what my son will look like. My mom had a c-section for the 3rd child. I prayed for no c-section during my pregnancy because the story I am about to share is the truth.

There was a white man named Tom. He was visiting the same church. He did something and was told not to come back ever again. These findings are later exposed. He gets close to the husband, and later, I will reveal why.

I used to go to a park in West Hartford and walk. It was a very beautiful place. I enjoyed the sights. We happened to see Tom, and there, I was in labor, starting to dilate. Tom is so into my baby who was not even born yet. We were not thinking about anything or being judgmental, but I was curious about the questions and declarations being said, so I walked away. He began to confide in the husband. He tells him more stuff, and the next thing I see is a check written out in my name and not the husband. It wasn't clear to me yet. A Check for $1,000.00 then he starts to say he will be born at 2 am in the morning. I am in labor, just walking to dilate more.

The Hospital

I got to the hospital, and they were trying to speed up the process. The assistant doctor came to the hospital wanting to do a c-section, and I was refusing to get that done. The doctor gave me a shot to slow down my heart rate to tell me that the baby was not going to make it normal, it had to be a c-section. He was just trying to get quick money because he was leaving for a retreat.

Confirmed later on, now I had caused a lot of madness. He had set up for a c-section, saying you and the baby are about to die and I started praying and speaking in tongues. Told the husband to call my real doctor. This assistant is not qualified to deliver this child. Get in that bathroom and pray and call the doctor, I kept saying. I kept telling him to not listen to this madman. He just put something in me to slow down my heart rate I said to my husband. All this happened around 4 am. Finally, my doctor arrived and checked me, and I was 10 centimeters ready to deliver. He tells his assistant to get the hell out of here and some other stuff. There was a crowd of nurses and doctors at my room doorway. So, they didn't go home until they saw what was going to happen. Some of them were calling me stupid, but I didn't care. I know prayers work, and I believed in my prayers. Amen. And I prevailed.

The Visitation

After all that, we still had the $1000 check, and my husband went to cash it, and it was a problem. Tom had to be called, I was still in my mind trying to find out what was his purpose behind this. We keep having these incidents. The husband wasn't working, and so he allowed Tom to take the family to eat out. Immanuel was a few weeks old now. On the way back, he asked me to take the scriptures off my windows and doors (I will explain that later). You going to have a visitation from the Lord, Tom said. I was like, what kind of visitation? He said you will see. So, we did what he said, and at midnight, there was a visitation. I have to say this, but a child was influenced, and I noticed that Spirit was after my son. He was sleeping so peacefully, but the Spirit wanted to wake him up, and I said No, that's it. I dealt with that Spirit for 6 hours, and I did not go to sleep until the host went to sleep then I grabbed my son, and I slept very lightly while everyone was snoring. I couldn't rest. I was searching for answers in my heart to my God.

Everything was quiet, and the Spirit was still in the apartment, but I prayed over the host, and now it was in the apartment, no host to work through. We haven't heard from Tom most of that day. Until I heard a song by Fred Hammond, and I ran around the apartment singing it, and then I played the song, and we all were in the living room singing, and singing with authority. The shade was down and that Spirit that visited flew out through the window. I know this is so true. Ten minutes later, Tom called and he said, God has promoted you as a Prophetess. Like what! Okay, I am just a little confused about how this went.

This was very new, and I was aware of my surroundings. I was a mother and daughter with no husband. I was not even accepted as the Elders, Deacons, and Pastor's children. I never felt accepted because I wasn't, and the pain you feel in that atmosphere is so hurtful. I was passed over in every way. To give an announcement in the church. I could only be in the choir and praise team. In this church, as a child, I ushered as well. I was in the children's choir and the Mass Choir, too. But when it came time for ministry I was not qualified. Lets me explain: I mentioned before I was a mother of 2 unmarried daughters. Were man's qualifications that I am not called or qualified for ministry, there is too much sin in my life, and God cannot be using someone like her.

Luke 23:34-35

34.Then Jesus said, "Father, forgive them, they know not what they do." They divided his garments by casting lots. 35. The people stood by and watched; the rulers, meanwhile, sneered at him and said, "He saved others. Let him save himself if he is the chosen one, the Messiah of God."

The Smell of the Presence of God

There is a presence, and it's called the presence of God. Many have not entered this phase yet. When you tap into heavenly places. Not just a good feel praise and audible worship. The experience is beyond that. It's a welcoming and warm presence that I am here with you, and you are not alone. It sometimes comes to give you protection, share a word of clarity, and maybe heal something in you or around you, which I call Revelation and Healing.

I am just praising around the apartment, singing no music. I always do it because I am mostly led by the Spirit of the Lord. I have no one to catch me when I fall out flat on the wood floor. Sometimes laid out for almost 1 hour and have never experienced any injuries. Can I get an Amen? My daughters just looking because they see me all the time.

In a nutshell, this kind of presence brings the smell of Olive Oil.

God's Presence with Olive Oil

Olive oil has been a symbol of God's presence and blessing throughout history, particularly in the Jewish and Christian traditions. The oil's significance is rooted in its use in religious rituals, its association with anointing and consecration, and its role as a symbol of divine grace and blessing.In the Old Testament, olive oil was used for a variety of religious purposes, including the anointing of the Tabernacle and its furnishings (Exodus 25:6), the consecration of Aaron and his sons as priests (Leviticus 8:30), and the purification of the Levites (Leviticus 16:32). The oil was also used in the lighting of the menorah in the tabernacle (Exodus 27:20) and in the anointing of kings and prophets (1 Samuel 16:13, 1 Kings 1:39)

In the New Testament, olive oil continues to play a significant role in the life of Jesus and the early Christian community. Jesus' mother, Mary, is said to have been presented with olive oil as a gift after his birth (Luke 2:36-38), and the oil was used in the anointing of Jesus' body before his burial (John 12:1-8). The early Christian community also used olive oil in the administration of the sacraments, particularly in the anointing of the sick and the consecration of altars (James 5:14, Hebrews 1:9)

Throughout history, olive oil has also been associated with the divine presence and the manifestation of God's power. In the Jewish tradition, the oil is seen as a symbol of the Shekinah, the divine presence that dwells among God's people. In the Christian tradition, the oil is associated with the Holy Spirit and the power of God's grace. In addition to its religious significance, olive oil has also played a practical role in the daily lives of Jews and Christians. The oil has been used for cooking, lighting, and medicinal purposes, and it has been a valuable commodity in many cultures. In conclusion, olive oil has been a symbol of God's presence and blessing throughout history, particularly in the Jewish and Christian traditions. The oil's significance is rooted in its use in religious rituals, its association with anointing and consecration, and its role as a symbol of divine grace and blessing.

The Praying for Comedians, Actors, Singers & Others

During my spiritual life and even now, I have had the opportunity to pray for certain famous people. That I was assigned to because it was out of the norm. Most of them I couldn't contact even though I tried to. But I just prayed as a leader and watched what God did for most of them that some may not even know that someone was even praying for them.

Suppose some of you are just like me in the background. You are as powerful and don't accept anything less. Keep doing what the God tells you to do. The only way to know is to do it. Learn your faults and your strengths. Your Pastor, bishop, or Apostle can only lead what he knows, and you can be higher than they are. Just because they have the title recognition and prophecy doesn't mean they are called ordained by God. You can be ordained by the Spirit of God. Being a spiritual person is not easy. Like I was trained by the Spirit of God. Man did not train me.

Covered my apartment with Bible Scriptures Windows and Doors

When I placed the scriptures on my windows and doors, I was led by the Holy Spirit, and just by obeying, my apartment was blessed and protected. The protection wasn't fully acknowledged until I was asked to take them down, as I explained in the visitation. I had friends spend the night, and they would have dreams or visions. You couldn't come and stay without receiving some kind of experience. This is the power of the scriptures; they speak, but you can't hear. The word is working for you all the time. Some people have closed Bibles at home. I leave mine open, so I know what to expect in the unexpected. I understand that some of us are taught to read the word out loud so it is heard. But the Bible is a protection; the WORDS are a protection against spirits you can see. If you read it or not. Open it up, and it will work for you. Lighting candles can't do what the Spirit of the Lord can. Do what you are led to do. To have visitations, dreams, and visions, you need to block all evil and negativity surrounding you.

Placing Bible scriptures on windows is a practice that some individuals and religious groups engage in to display their faith and share religious messages with others. This practice can be seen in various contexts, including homes, churches, and other places of worship.

The act of placing Bible scriptures on windows can serve multiple purposes. Firstly, it can be a personal expression of faith and a reminder of one's beliefs. By displaying verses from the Bible, individuals can surround themselves with words of inspiration, encouragement, and guidance. It can also serve as a visual representation of one's commitment to living according to the teachings of the Bible.

In addition to personal reasons, placing Bible scriptures on windows can also be a way to share one's faith with others. By making these verses visible to those passing by or entering the space, individuals hope to spark curiosity, initiate conversations about religion, or simply provide a source of comfort and inspiration to others.

There are various ways in which people choose to display Bible scriptures on windows. Some individuals may use window decals or stickers specifically designed for this purpose. These decals often feature popular verses or quotes from the Bible and can be easily applied and removed from windows without causing damage. Others may choose to write or paint verses directly onto the glass using special markers or paints that are designed for use on windows. This allows for more customization and creativity in the presentation of the scriptures.

It is important to note that the practice of placing Bible scriptures on windows is not universally practiced or endorsed by all Christian denominations or religious groups. The decision to engage in this practice is often based on personal preference and interpretation of religious teachings.

Some individuals may find comfort and inspiration in having Bible verses displayed prominently in their living spaces or places of worship. They may see it as creating an environment that is infused with spiritual significance and reminders of their faith. Placing Bible scriptures on windows can also serve as a visual reminder of the importance of incorporating religious teachings into one's daily life.

However, it is essential to respect the beliefs and practices of others when it comes to displaying religious symbols or texts in shared spaces. In some cases, there may be restrictions or guidelines in place regarding the use of religious imagery or messages in public or communal areas. It is always advisable to consult with relevant authorities or seek guidance from religious leaders before engaging in practices that may affect others or violate any regulations.

In conclusion, placing Bible scriptures on windows is a personal and often meaningful practice for individuals who wish to display their faith and share religious messages with others. It can serve as a reminder of one's beliefs, a source of inspiration, and a way to initiate conversations about religion. However, it is important to consider the context and respect the beliefs and practices of others when engaging in this practice.

Desert Storm, January 16, 1991-

While in college in 1990, before Thanksgiving, many of my male friends who signed up for G-loan were drafted out of college. Many of them came to me for prayer as they feared leaving, while some were excited about the experience. I prayed for all who came to me.

In 1991, just settling in Atlanta, GA, I was 19. I remember going to sleep, and I dreamed. Maybe I don't make sense. But, I dreamed that I was trying to wake up President Bush and let him know the war had just started while he was sleeping. This was in January 1991, and I saw a stand with a red button. I have never been to the white house. I woke up and shared it with a roommate.

That morning, the news came out, and it said 'President Bush asleep during the start of the war.' Now, you know I was shocked. I just shared this with 2 young ladies this morning. Because it was on the news it came to pass what I had saw. One of the ladies reported this to the upper staff. I was called a witch, a demon and was immediately kicked out and turned homeless.

Operation Desert Storm began 31 years ago — on January 16, 1991 — five months after Iraqi forces invaded and annexed Kuwait. That operation to oust the Iraqis is also known as the Gulf War; it came about after Iraqi President Saddam Hussein refused to withdraw his forces from Kuwait.

Susan Smith – October 1994

I am a single mother raising 2 lovely girls. And I was taking very good care of them. Bringing them to church. I always tried to maintain a car so that I could take them to places. I loved my girls and wouldn't want anything to happen to them. I wouldn't hurt my girls in any circumstance, not even for a man.

Every night, I would read my Bible, then pray and check on my girls before I went to bed. This was my regular routine. On this particular night, I was dreaming. I saw that I got up and dressed my daughters. My youngest asked, 'Mommy, where are we going?' I said, 'for a ride.' We got into my car, and I strapped them tight in the seat belts. I then drove to Kenny Park, where there was a lake. I kissed both my girls, let the car go into the lake, and watched it sink.

I woke up sweating, looked around my bedroom in so much fear, jumped out of my bed, ran down the hall to the girl's room, and they were still in their bed; that was a great relief. I just said, 'ok, it was a dream from the enemy,' and went back to sleep. This was around 2am-3am in the morning.

I remember watching the news with my grandmother. Breaking news appeared addressing a mother of 2 boys. Saying a black man with a hat on had pulled her out of the car and stole it with the boys in the back seat.

I immediately said to my Grandmother I think that lady is lying, not knowing that this is the lady that I dreamed about drowning her sons. So, we continued to watch the news about this as they looked for this black man. It came out that she confessed to killing her sons by drowning in a car. A dream I witnessed myself.

In 1994, Susan Smith was convicted of murdering her two young sons, three-year-old Michael, and 14-month-old Alexander, by drowning them in a South Carolina lake.

September 11, 2001

September 10, 2001, was the beginning of a history of sorrow for many and the USA as a whole.

I remember this day as it happened yesterday. Living in a shelter for families sponsored by the Salvation Army Fort Lauderdale. I started a cleaning business named "Clean-it-All," an all-cleaning service for living in a shelter and cleaning homes.

On that morning of September 10, busy as usual getting the boys ready for daycare and the girls for school. It was a normal time for us. We go out cleaning. Now picking the boys up for daycare. We go to Publix grocery to buy groceries for dinner. In the checkout line, there were 2 Muslim-looking men in behind us, smiling at my boys. Seemed so innocent and nice. I smiled back and was very friendly, and so were they.

After going back home, cooking dinner and settling the kids down, a few hours later, I started to feel sorrow in my entire being, and the song "I love York" began to flow in my mind and thoughts. My husband at the time asked me 'am I ok?' and I said 'no.' Because I feel like something bad is about to happen in New York.

My mom lived in Brooklyn at the time. I called her and asked, 'what's going on?' She said 'nothing.' But shared with me that my brother was going for a welding job somewhere in Manhattan. I told her to tell him not to go because something is going to happen, and I don't know what exactly. I continued to pray that night and went to sleep after my heart and mind released me.

September 11, 2001, I wake up as usual, with the same routine: got the kids ready for daycare and school and went to clean some homes. After dropping the boys off to daycare, we went to clean a home. This home was not far from the FLL, and I always loved to see the planes take off when they did. But this particular morning, before turning on the radio or seeing the news. I noticed that the planes were not taking off. And immediately, I was somewhat worried that it was not New York, maybe here in Florida.

To get clarity, I turned on the radio, and what I felt was correct was the New York Twin Towers. I was in total shock that I had witnessed such an experience again. But, this time, it involved the loss of so many lives.

So, I saw a great standstill in America. I was so shocked I couldn't clean any homes the rest of the day. My husband brought me back home, and he went to pick up the boys from daycare. As I sat glued to my chair for the next hours, I watched the news of the 2nd plane crashing into the Twin Towers. Watching people jumping out the windows. I couldn't stop crying. I watched it until the end.

Isaiah 41:10

Fear thou not; for I am with thee: be not dismayed; for I am thy God: I will strengthen thee; yea, I will help thee; yea, I will uphold thee with the right hand of my righteousness.

Romans 12:21

Be not overcome of evil but overcome evil with good.

On September 11, 2001, terrorists killed nearly 3,000 people and injured more than 6,000 others in the worst attack on the homeland in our nation's history. In New York City!

Sandy Hook- School shooting 2012 Connecticut

On December 1, 2012, A clear day in Florida. I was confused by a dream I just had. The location was so close. I meditated on it because it was a reminder of similar dreams and events encountered. This was a school shooting, and even though I heard so much about these tragic events happening, this was close to home. As I was thinking about the tragic school shooting I had in my dream, my younger daughter said, Mommy, I had a dream about a school shooting, and we talked about it, and we saw the same event and had different experiences and views.

I was immediately compelled to list it on my Facebook page. Didn't fully understand it at first, but I felt that it needed to be shared. Days went by, and no one responded. It was just a dream, and I'll just keep praying. Just moving forward and watching my life struggle after losing my sons. Their father kidnapped them from me and spread lies. It was rough, and thinking about how I could get my sons back. How can God be using me? And I am heartbroken about my sons and fearing their upbringing.

On December 14, 2012.

The Sandy Hook Elementary School shooting was a mass shooting that occurred on December 14, 2012, in Newtown, Connecticut, United States, when 20-year-old Adam Lanza shot and killed 26 people. Twenty of the victims were children between six and seven years old, and the other six were adult staff members.

Myles Monroe – 2014

Myles Munroe, OBE, was a Bahamian evangelist and ordained minister, avid professor of the Kingdom of God, author, speaker, and leadership consultant. He founded and led the Bahamas Faith Ministries International and Myles Munroe International.

In my awakened state, I was in the guard shack at work in Washington State. Sitting in the I went into an open vision and saw a small private jet burst into flames. I began to feel like a sadness came upon me and I called a friend and shared it with her. Then I was led to my Facebook and got the news. When I opened my Facebook page, I saw Creflo Dollar's post (My condolence to the Munroe Family), and I was shocked. That really hit me because I saw the crash, and I just began to pray.

When God is using you, there are people who don't understand, and it makes the environment very uncomfortable. You really can have a language with negative people when it comes to people that in the history.

2 Corinthians 8:9 King James Version

9 For ye know the grace of our Lord Jesus Christ, that, though he was rich, yet for your sakes he became poor, that ye through his poverty might be rich.

Yellow Cab Dispatcher Overnight

In 1998, working at Yellow Cab overnight shift. This particular night, it was busy in Fort Lauderdale, Florida. I had always locked my van with the lock over the steering wheel. I had my break around 3 am and forgot to put it on. Almost time to go home, but there was an incident, and I wasn't fully aware of it until I went outside. There were police, and older Black females were robbed. And had stolen my Dodge caravan.

So, I am really calm about this. I was asked questions I couldn't answer because I was working. I don't know many people; I am just moving here from Connecticut. And it was sad because I had 4 children, and 2 were in car seats the shelter had supplied to us. After the police questioning, I was looking for answers my mind acted accordingly. There was a white car with tinted windows, and it was running and I notice it and the police didn't. I alerted a police officer about the running car. It had been abandoned, maybe by the people who stole my minivan. They searched and took fingerprints. And I was given a ride home and a number. Also, I was told I just have to face the fact that I won't find my van, and it is a part of a criminal case. What a wake-up call!

Yep, prayer is the key. Within 2 weeks, my van was found, and I was alerted. It was still in the same condition, and the police were kind of shocked, but I wasn't. I prayed and knew it would be alright after paying fees to get my van, yes. I had to pay a fee, and I was the victim. A week later, I was on my way to work at Ford of Pompano as a cashier. My back window has been busted a broken into pieces. This was the cause of the woman attacked and robbed who had accused my sons, who were aged 6 months and 14 months, of attacking their mom. This was what the family was saying, and they tried to charge me. Later on, I was already in a shelter, and funds were low. And now had to fix a back window of a minivan. I believe this case was closed, and the people got caught. I didn't stay long in the yellow cab after this incident.

Ford of Pompano 2000

Ford of Pompano, I was just getting started and liked the job. Before I go into detail please understand this is a true experience as the other stories. My background of working with money. From the age of 10 I was working in school the school store. Where I am responsible for getting everything together. Pack up, set up and put back where it belongs. I was the school store manager, and I was good at what I did. My motto was no money, no product. Selling school supplies. Most of my jobs started as work-study jobs, and those dollars helped me through my entire school adventure. Just to say, I worked as a cashier at a few grocery stores, and I know how to count money, so counting was not an issue for me. I have worked at Super Stop & Shop, Mcdonalds, Burger King, Wendy's and Krystal and never had a money issue.

I wasn't at the Ford of Pompano for long because the lady who was training me was stilling the money under my cashier number because she was training me. I think it was about $1500.00. I was short on the days she was training me. She has been there 3 years I believe. So, $1500. X 4 or more. I would have fired me, too. But I wasn't stealing and got fired. I tried to tell the ugly black man looking at me funny for days. He judged me because I was living in a shelter.

Isaiah 43:2

When you pass through the waters, I will be with you; and when you pass through the rivers, they will not sweep over you. When you walk through the fire, you will not be burned; the flames will not set you ablaze.

Psalm 45:7

You have loved righteousness and hated wickedness;

Therefore God, Your God, has anointed You

With the oil of joy above Your fellows.

Isaiah 43:18-19 King James Version (KJV)

Behold, I will do a new thing; now it shall spring forth; shall ye not know it? I will even make a way in the wilderness, and rivers in the desert.

Matthew says that the birth of Jesus by the Virgin Mary is to "fulfill what the Lord had spoken by the prophet: 'Behold, the virgin shall conceive and bear a son, and they shall call his name Immanuel' (which means, God with us)" (1:22-23).

Acts 2:17 NIV"'In the last days, God says, I will pour out my Spirit on all people. Your sons and daughters will prophesy, your young men will see visions, your old men will dream dreams.

Romans 9:17

For the scripture saith unto Pharaoh, Even for this same purpose have I raised thee up, that I might shew my power in thee, and that my name might be declared throughout all the earth.

Deuteronomy 18:18 King James Version

18 I will raise them up a Prophet from among their brethren, like unto thee, and will put my words in his mouth; and he shall speak unto them all that I shall command him.

Psalm 105:15 King James Version

15 Saying, Touch not mine anointed, and do my prophets no harm.

I am the Isaiah 61 Prophet for my Generation

61 The Spirit of the Lord God is upon me; because the Lord hath anointed me to preach good tidings unto the meek; he hath sent me to bind up the brokenhearted,

to proclaim liberty to the captives, and the opening of the prison to them that are bound;

2 To proclaim the acceptable year of the Lord, and the day of vengeance of our God; to comfort all that mourn;

3 To appoint unto them that mourn in Zion, to give unto them beauty for ashes, the oil of joy for mourning, the garment of praise for the sSpiritof heaviness; that they might be called trees of righteousness, the planting of the Lord, that he might be glorified.

4 And they shall build the old wastes, they shall raise up the former desolations, and they shall repair the waste cities, the desolations of many generations.

5 And strangers shall stand and feed your flocks, and the sons of the alien shall be your plowmen and your vinedressers.

6 But ye shall be named the Priests of the Lord: men shall call you the Ministers of our God: ye shall eat the riches of the Gentiles, and in their glory shall ye boast yourselves.

7 For your shame ye shall have double; and for confusion they shall rejoice in their portion: therefore in their land they shall possess the double: everlasting joy shall be unto them.

8 For I the Lord love judgment, I hate robbery for burnt offering; and I will direct their work in truth, and I will make an everlasting covenant with them.

9 And their seed shall be known among the Gentiles, and their offspring among the people: all that see them shall acknowledge them, that they are the seed which the Lord hath blessed.

10 I will greatly rejoice in the Lord, my soul shall be joyful in my God; for he hath clothed me with the garments of salvation, he hath covered me with the robe of righteousness, as a bridegroom decketh himself with ornaments, and as a bride adorneth herself with her jewels.

11 For as the earth bringeth forth her bud, and as the garden causeth the things that are sown in it to spring forth; so the Lord God will cause righteousness and praise to spring forth before all the nations.

Walmart Unfairness 2003 - 2008

Working in Walmart 2003-2005 overnight cashier, prior to getting hired, I had to take a pathological test which I failed 3 or 4 times. It kept saying I was lying when I was telling the truth but after a few attempts he approved and I was hired.

One night I was on my menstrual cycle. I had my lunch break and I didn't have much winter clothing so I decided to shop for some sweatpants and shirts to work in. I carried my backpack the entire time. After I paid for my stuff one of the assistant mgr. came and approached me. He wanted to check my bag and I said ok. He was quite out of order and was profiling me. The next morning when the store manager arrived, I immediately went to her and explained what had happened.

One evening at work the CSM approached me and asked, "Charmaine how much are you being paid?" I told her the amount and she shared with me about the overnight differential pay I was not getting paid for. She also talked about how I already know how to do everything, how I come to work on time, and that I don't call out. The next day when I got off, I decided to go to the office and talk to the HR in the store. They told me that it wasn't the truth and that I was getting the right amount of pay. I said it wasn't true and then I left. I called the headquarters in Arkansas and asked for the wage department's Human Resource Manager

and only told him the store, city-state, and my first &
last name.

This was my first year at Hallandale Beach
Walmart.

The store manager at that time was from Okee-
chobee Walmart and I was not fully aware if I would
receive all my money. I didn't miss any days during
that time.

Walmart Oakland Park Roof caves in:

I was on my way to work; the hurricane winds
were strong. As I was driving, I had a feeling of turning around and going back home, and I am glad I did
because the roof of my store collapsed.

We were all sent to different stores to work after
the incident. I ended up at Pompano Beach Walmart
and started as a cashier during the day. Overnight
wasn't available yet. I waited until overnight was
available.

I nearly worked every Dept. and with perfection .

Got everything done I started.

Becoming a CSM

For some of the daytime CSMs, who were already
on the floor, I used to help them. It was just that. Then,
I was asked to apply but only one position was open,
Another person was training too but did not take the
test. I spoke to the Asst. Mgr. O. about the position and

he looked at me like "NO" and then he went on to say, "You are too nice" to become a CSM. He then watched me all night and it was a little uncomfortable. I was already nervous. A customer came through and as I can remember, she took off her skirt in front of the register. It was funny too. Then he said, "Go for it!"

Excited, on my very next day off, I went to Walmart to take the test and get an oil change. I passed the test as competitive and the other lady failed.

Before I got the Customer Service Manager position. it was not easy but when God orders your feet, it is settled. My Apostle at the time might have seen the position of the CSM before I got it because there was someone against it. But what God has for you, that is for you.

Some things that happened that were unfair, very

unfair.

In the oil change I got, the oil cap was not put on tight and the oil spilled out ruining my transmission. I went to the Store Mgr. but because I was an employee, they refused to fix it. I ended up fixing it for $3000 and then didn't put the freon in it.

One morning I was driving all the children to their school. The last one was baby Joshua. As I was turning, the steering wheel locked on me on the turn and the car headed towards a black fence. I was so scared but I hit the brakes and stopped in time to turn the steering wheel in position to drive. I had to go get a new car which was my last choice, especially with 5 children to drive.

I went to Toyota of Hollywood with my minivan. I had no cash to pick out a new car so I chose a 2007 Toyota Corolla 5 speed. My trade was for $4000 and I wrote two $500 post-dated cheques because Walmart paid every 2 weeks.

I got to work and another CSM asked me how much money I put down and I said my van was the trade for $4000.

The next day in the afternoon, I got a call from Hollywood Toyota asking me and my husband to come there. I didn't understand why he wanted both of us, I didn't have him as a co-signer.

We arrived at the dealership. The salesperson greeted us and people were looking at us very strangely. He said that someone called from Walmart and asked how much money I put into the car. He replied to them "You didn't put no cash down," which was correct. We didn't know what to think of this occurrence.

That night I went in to work and about 15 minutes in, I was called back. I had an idea why but after being alerted by the dealership they were saying that "$4000 dollars was missing." I am looking like

"What is the issue I haven't taken anything." The Store Manager asked, "You have a new car?" I replied, "Yes, but I had my car before this happened. And I didn't put any cash down." This was bad, very bad. They could not prove I took it because I didn't.

Ever since then, they put that in their records despite it not being true and it followed me all the way to Fort Pierce Walmart. That lie!

I was moving to Port Saint Lucie because every time I traveled through, felt like home to me in 1998. I was just traveling for vacation but that city stuck with me out of all the other cities in Florida.

In 2007 we moved to PSL. We rented a 3-bedroom house and waited till our home was built. Maronda homes 5/2.5, 2-story view from I-95 even this day. Living in PSL, I drove back and forth to Pompano Beach working 4 pm-4 am. I was a very good CSM. I was preparing shifts. Everything was very good, things got done. Until I got accepted into Fort Pierce Walmart. I hate to say what I am about to say but it is true. It was a set-up to get rid of me within a year because of that $4000 that I didn't take. But I had a new car. Well planned by the thief who ruined a job I could have still been working because I loved working there and I was good at it too.

I don't do drama. I come to do a job, never looking for sexual relationships. I was firm about this. I still could see that Asst. Mgr. G looking at me like I was a snack. I hated but I still had to be friendly and cordial because he oversaw the overnight shift. I later found out that he was hired to watch me and catch me stealing. I had a feeling about this and before he made his move, he said he was sorry about what he was about to do. That was in September 2008 and because of the lies from the other Walmart Store.

I can tell you something innocent can be taken wrong. I was confused about the plot against me because the female involved was married, he had a girlfriend, and I was married as well. I was framed for something I had no clarity. I was fired and lied about in multiple ways a person can imagine and I believe they added stealing money too. Wow! They were determined to frame me for something I didn't do in the first place.

After, this it was hard to find a job. I lost the car and then the home. It was a very bad experience for me. I was totally innocent.

Drug Abuse Treatment Association

The unfairness in this workplace.

I started in this company on 7/2016 and ended on 7/31/2023. The starting pay was $10, the end pay was $15 and after I quit, some were given $17 and $19 just like it was shown to me. I was truly fed up and not looking back. I have worked and did my job. Alarms were turned off and they always tried to set me up. I was refused weekends off even after 6 years and they hired new people who easily got weekends off. It was just an unorganized company. I was cheated hours and they only paid me for the 10 hours after all the overtime. I realized I had been missing hours for years.

FEDEX – February 16, 2022,

I was hired at FedEx as a packer. The hours weren't promised as agreed. I was hired for at least 15 hours with the option to add more but they were not always available. I was injured on the job while working in a loading truck alone and no one checked on me. That wasn't the first time I was in a loading truck alone. I was always careful because I didn't want to get injured. That would not be a good thing for me. I was single and had to take care of myself. My injuries were sprained ankle and knee.

One day, I came into work a little late and I asked if could I go to malls because I had signed up for it. I was told no and I just went to the department. I was told to go load the truck and that's what I did. I am about 30-45 min. on the clock for a box to load it, trying to secure myself. I put my foot(right) between a part of the package slide. As I reached thinking I had secured myself, my left foot slipped down on the left which caused my right foot to get stuck and I immediately pulled myself up with my hands to stop further twisting my knee and ankle. My right foot was still on the slide and I had to pull it out for which I am grateful. I endured the pain for a few minutes. I had to force myself out of the truck. No one checked on me even when I called for help. The noise was too loud for anyone to hear me. I thought the camera would have seen me.

That's what happened. Next, I was not surprised due to my previous work encounters, as this had already happened and no one believed me. I have never sued anyone before but I was fed up with all this workplace stuff. I am a hard-working honest person who is not lazy and works as hard as everyone else.

This is my point – Wrongful Termination/Signature Forgery

I was injured and yet complied with the rules. There are three people involved in getting me fired. I did not understand the integrity of the company when it came to writing signatures. I thought a signature was a person's first and last name. This was a mistake and it needed to be clarified but no lawyer wanted to take my case. My granddaughter's father who was also working at FEDEX had told me about the job. Since I have had experience in a warehouse and needed more money, I applied. Scott, later on, wanted to do more hours and we talked about it. I then spoke to the supervisor in the office. He replied with "If Scott wants to work more hours, you can switch to part-time." He encouraged me to sign a paper which he said he would hold until I made a decision. I told him I would not put my signature until I heard further notice from Scott but Scott changed his mind and quit instead. I went to the office and asked back for the paper but he refused to give it to me. I thought, because there was no signature completed, I was ok. Who signed the my full signature? Only the letter C was left. Not my whole name was signed on that sheet. I didn't quit but, going through this experience let's say never again and the lawyers made sure of that in writing.

I was told to sign up for shifts. I did that a few times but then they were deleted. I called and I was told again to sign up for shift on the app which I did time after time again, until I realized that my account was closed a month later. I did not know what happened but instinct told me to screenshot the refusal of shift and who authorized it. Then I saw the mail and the reason for the termination and I was SMH. I was just fed up with workplaces and I realized that it's just not for me. They got away with it and the lawyers will have their day. Amen.

Joshua was born during Hurricane Ivan in 2004. The lady in my room stole my $300 which was for his circumcision and pictures.

Salvation Army Christmas 2001

The Salvation Army Christmas story - Making a dream come true was a good thing until the deception and lies to the world. Telling TBN about how many kids we have. I do believe there was a man who had written us a check to buy a home but then they were trying to kick us out. We never received it.

Delta Airline Airport Security-

Hartsfield International Airport

I was pregnant and they fired me during my first pregnancy and when I was in pain, on my birthday. I had to call out.

I have had opportunities to meet and shake the hands of Jesse Jackson.

I have seen Emmanuel Lewis (who plays "Webster" in a TV show)

FEMA-2008- 2014

I had a great experience. I prayed for many people and hoped everything came to pass.

By Charmaine Overton